The Gardener's

BOOK OF POEMS
AND POESIES

The Gardener's BOOK OF POEMS AND POESIES

COMPILED BY CARY O. YAGER

CONTEMPORARY BOOKS

A TRIBUNE NEW MEDIA/EDUCATION COMPANY

Library of Congress Cataloging-in-Publication Data

The gardener's book of poems and poesies.
          p.   cm.
     ISBN 0-8092-3217-0
     1. Gardens—Poetry.   2. Gardening—Poetry.
     3. Nature—Poetry.
     PN6110.G2G32   1996
     808.81'936—dc20   95-51235
                                                  CIP

Copyright © 1996 by Contemporary Books, Inc.
Published by Contemporary Books, Inc.
Two Prudential Plaza, Chicago, Illinois 60601-6790
Manufactured in the United States of America
International Standard Book Number: 0-8092-3217-0
10   9   8   7   6   5   4   3   2   1

To Linda and Patsy

Acknowledgments

"Afternoon on a Hill" by Edna St. Vincent Millay. From *Collected Poems* by Edna St. Vincent Millay, published by HarperCollins. Copyright 1917, 1945 by Edna St. Vincent Millay.

"April" by Sara Teasdale. Reprinted with the permission of Simon & Schuster from *The Collected Poems of Sara Teasdale* (New York: Macmillan, 1937).

"April Rain Song" by Langston Hughes. From *The Dream Keeper and Other Poems* by Langston Hughes. Copyright 1932 by Alfred A. Knopf, Inc., and renewed 1960 by Langston Hughes. Reprinted by permission of the publisher.

From "The Burning of the Leaves" by Laurence Binyon. Reprinted by permission of Mrs. Nicolete Gray and the Society of Authors on behalf of the Laurence Binyon Estate.

"Child on Top of a Greenhouse" by Theodore Roethke. Copyright 1946 by Editorial Publications, Inc. From The *Collected Poems of Theodore Roethke* by Theodore Roethke. Used by permission of Doubleday, a division of Bantam Doubleday Dell Publishing Group, Inc.

"Fireflies in the Garden" by Robert Frost. From *The Poetry of Robert Frost*, edited by Edward Connery Lathem. Copyright © 1956 by Robert Frost. Copyright 1928, 1969 by Henry Holt and Co., Inc. Reprinted by permission of Henry Holt and Co., Inc.

"The First Blue-Bird" by James Whitcomb Riley. Reprinted with permission of Simon & Schuster from *The Complete Works of James Whitcomb Riley* (New York: Macmillan, 1913).

The Garden

Andrew Marvell
1621–1678

How vainly men themselves amaze,
To win the palm, the oak, or bays,
And their incessant labors see
Crowned from some single herb or tree
Whose short and narrow-vergèd shade
Does prudently their toils upbraid,
While all the flowers and trees do close
To weave the garlands of repose!

Fair quiet, have I found thee here,
And Innocence, thy sister dear?
Mistaken long, I sought you then
In busy companies of men.
Your sacred plants, if here below,
Only among the plants will grow;
Society is all but rude
To this delicious solitude.

No white nor red was ever seen
So amorous as this lovely green.
Fond lovers, cruel as their flame,
Cut in these trees their mistress' name.

Little, alas! they know or heed,
How far these beauties hers exceed!
Fair trees! where'se'er your bark I wound,
No name shall but your own be found.

When we have run our passion's heat,
Love hither makes his best retreat.
The gods, that mortal beauty chase,
Still in a tree did end their race:
Apollo hunted Daphne so,
Only that she might laurel grow;
And Pan did after Syrinx speed,
Not as a nymph, but for a reed.

What wondrous life is this I lead!
Ripe apples drop about my head;
The luscious clusters of the vine
Upon my mouth do crush their wine;
The nectarine, and curious peach,
Into my hands themselves do reach;
Stumbling on melons, as I pass,
Insnared with flowers, I fall on grass.

Meanwhile the mind, from pleasure less,
Withdraws into its happiness;—
The mind, that ocean where each kind
Does straight its own resemblance find;
Yet it creates, transcending these,
Far other worlds, and other seas,

Annihilating all that's made
To a green thought in a green shade.

Here at the fountain's sliding foot,
Or at some fruit-tree's mossy root,
Casting the body's vest aside,
My soul into the boughs does glide:
There, like a bird, it sits and sings,
Then whets and combs its silver wings,
And, till prepared for longer flight,
Waves in its plumes the various light.

Such was that happy garden-state,
While man there walked without a mate:
After a place so pure and sweet,
What other help could yet be meet!
But 'twas beyond a mortal's share
To wander solitary there:
Two paradises 'twere in one,
To live in paradise alone.

How well the skillful gardener drew
Of flowers, and herbs, this dial new;
Where, from above, the milder sun
Does through a fragrant zodiac run,
And, as it works, the industrious bee
Computes its time as well as we!
How could such sweet and wholesome hours
Be reckoned but with herbs and flowers?

My Garden

Thomas Edward Brown
1830–1897

A garden is a lovesome thing, God wot!
Rose plot,
Fringed pool,
Ferned grot—
The veriest school
Of peace; and yet the fool
Contends that God is not—
Not God! in gardens! when the eve is cool?
Nay, but I have a sign;
'Tis very sure God walks in mine.

I Went Out into the Garden

Moses Ibn Ezra
1060–1138

I went out into the garden in the morning
    dusk,
When sorrow enveloped me like a cloud;
And the breeze brought to my nostril the
    odor of spices,
As balm of healing for a sick soul—
Then a sudden dawn flamed in the sky, like
    lightning,
And its thunder surged like the cry of a
    woman that gives birth!

Translated by Solomon Solis-Cohen

From *"Spring"*

James Thomson the Elder
1700–1748

At length the finished garden to the view
Its vistas open and its alleys green.
Snatched through the verdant maze, the
   hurried eye
Distracted wanders; now the bowery walk
Of covert close, where scarce a speck of day
Falls on the lengthened gloom, protracted
   sweeps;
Now meets the bending sky, the river now
Dimpling along, the breezy ruffled lake,
The forest darkening round, the glittering
   spire,
The ethereal mountain, and the distant
   main.
But why so far excursive? when at hand,
Along these blushing borders bright with
   dew,
And in yon mingled wilderness of flowers,
Fair-handed Spring unbosoms every
   grace—
Throws out the snow-drop and the crocus
   first,

The daisy, primrose, violet darkly blue,
And polyanthus of unnumbered dyes;
The yellow wall-flower, stained with iron
     brown,
And lavish stock, that scents the garden
     round:
From the soft wing of vernal breezes shed,
Anemones, auriculas, enriched
With shining meal o'er all their velvet leaves;
And full ranunculus of glowing red.
Then comes the tulip-race, where beauty
     plays
Her idle freaks: from family diffused
To family, as flies the father-dust,
The varied colours run; and, while they
     break,
On the charmed eye, the exulting florist
     marks
With secret pride the wonders of his hand.
No gradual bloom is wanting—from the bud
First-born of Spring to Summer's musky
     tribes;
Nor hyacinths, of purest virgin white,
Low bent and blushing inward; nor jonquils,
Of potent fragrance; nor narcissus fair,
As o'er the fabled fountain hanging still;
Nor broad carnations, nor gay-spotted pinks;

Nor, showered from every bush, the damask-
   rose:
Infinite numbers, delicacies, smells.
With hues on hues expression cannot paint,
The breath of Nature, and her endless
   bloom.

In the Spring

From "The Greek Anthology"

Meleager

75 B.C.–?

Now the bright crocus flames, and now
    The slim narcissus takes the rain,
And, straying o'er the mountain's brow,
    The daffodillies bud again.
The thousand blossoms wax and wane
    On wold, and heath, and fragrant bough,
    But fairer than the flowers art thou
Than any growth of hill or plain.

Ye gardens cast your leafy crown,
That my love's feet may tread it down,
    Like lilies on the lilies set;
My Love, whose lips are softer far
Than drowsy poppy petals are,
    And sweeter than the violet!

Translated by Andrew Lang

Ode on the Spring

Thomas Gray
1716–1771

Lo! where the rosy-bosom'd Hours,
  Fair Venus' train, appear,
Disclose the long-expecting flowers
  And wake the purple year!
The Attic warbler pours her throat
Responsive to the cuckoo's note,
The untaught harmony of Spring:
While, whispering pleasure as they fly,
Cool Zephyrs thro' the clear blue sky
  Their gather'd fragrance fling.

Where'er the oak's thick branches stretch
  A broader, browner shade,
Where'er the rude and moss-grown beech
  O'er-canopies the glade,
Beside some water's rushy brink
With me the Muse shall sit, and think
(At ease reclined in rustic state)
How vain the ardour of the Crowd,
How low, how little are the Proud,
  How indigent the Great!

Still is the toiling hand of Care;
    The panting herds repose:
Yet hark, how thro' the peopled air
    The busy murmur glows!
The insect youth are on the wing,
Eager to taste the honied spring
And float amid the liquid noon:
Some lightly o'er the current skim,
Some show their gaily-gilded trim
    Quick-glancing to the sun.

To Contemplation's sober eye
    Such is the race of Man:
And they that creep, and they that fly,
    Shall end where they began.
Alike the busy and the gay
But flutter thro' life's little day,
In Fortune's varying colours drest:
Brush'd by the hand of rough Mischance,
Or chill'd by Age, their airy dance
    They leave, in dust to rest.

Methinks I hear in accents low
    The sportive kind reply:
Poor moralist! and what art thou?
    A solitary fly!
Thy joys no glittering female meets,
No hive hast thou of hoarded sweets,

No painted plumage to display:
On hasty wings thy youth is flown;
Thy sun is set, thy spring is
    gone—
    We frolic while 'tis May.

Now the Lusty Spring

From "The Tragedy
of Valentinian"

John Fletcher
1579–1625

Now the lusty spring is seen;
   Golden yellow, gaudy blue,
   Daintily invite the view.
Everywhere on every green,
Roses blushing as they blow,
   And enticing men to pull,
Lilies whiter than the snow,
   Woodbines of sweet honey full:
      All love's emblems, and all cry,
      "Ladies, if not plucked, we die."

Yet the lusty spring hath stayed;
   Blushing red and purest white
   Daintily to love invite
Every woman, every maid.

Cherries kissing as they grow,
  And inviting men to taste,
Apples even ripe below,
  Winding gently to the waist:
    All love's emblems, and all cry,
    "Ladies, if not plucked, we die."

The Innocent Spring

Edith Sitwell
1887–1964

In the great gardens, after bright spring
   rain,
We find sweet innocence come once again,
White periwinkles, little pensionnaires,
With muslin gowns and shy and candid airs,

That under saint-blue skies, with gold stars
   sown,
Hide their sweet innocence by spring winds
   blown,
From zephyr libertines that like Richelieu
And d'Orsay their gold-spangled kisses blew;

And lilies of the valley whose buds blonde
   and tight
Seem curls of little school-children that
   light
The priests' procession, when on some saint's
   day
Along the country paths they make their
   way;

Forget-me-nots, whose eyes of childish blue,
Gold-starred like heaven, speak of love still
    true;
And all the flowers that we call "dear heart,"
Who say their prayers like children, then
    depart

Into the dark. Amid the dew's bright beams
The summer airs, like Weber waltzes, fall
Round the first rose who, flushed with her
    youth, seems
Like a young Princess dressed for her first
    ball.

Who knows what beauty ripens from dark
    mould
After the sad wind and the winter's cold?—
But a small wind sighed, colder than the
    rose
Blooming in desolation, "No one knows."

Sweetly Breathing, Vernal Air

Thomas Carew
1595?–1645?

Sweetly breathing, vernal air,
That with kind warmth doth repair
Winter's ruins; from whose breast
All the gums and spice of the East
Borrow their perfumes; whose eye
Gilds the morn, and clears the sky.
Whose dishevelled tresses shed
Pearls upon the violet bed;
On whose brow, with calm smiles drest
The halcyon sits and builds her nest;
Beauty, youth, and endless spring
Dwell upon thy rosy wing!
Thou, if stormy Boreas throws
Down whole forests when he blows,
With a pregnant, flowery birth,
Canst refresh the teeming earth.
If he nip the early bud,
If he blast what's fair or good,
If he scatter our choice flowers,
If he shake our halls or bowers,

If his rude breath threaten us,
Thou canst stroke great Æolus,
And from him the grace obtain,
To bind him in an iron chain.

Give Me the
Splendid Silent Sun

Walt Whitman
1819–1892

Give me the splendid silent sun with all its
beams full-dazzling,
Give me juicy autumnal fruit ripe and red
from the orchard,
Give me a field where the unmowed grass
grows,
Give me an arbor, give me the trellised
grape,
Give me fresh corn and wheat, give me
serene-moving animals teaching content.
Give me nights perfectly quiet as on high
plateaus west of the Mississippi, and I am
looking up at the stars,
Give me odorous at sunrise a garden of
beautiful flowers where I can walk
undisturbed.

Thaw

Edward Thomas
1878–1917

Over the land freckled with snow half-
  thawed
The speculating rooks at their nests cawed
And saw from elm-tops, delicate as flower of
  grass,
What we below could not see, Winter pass.

April

Sara Teasdale
1884–1933

The roofs are shining from the rain,
    The sparrows twitter as they fly,
And with a windy April grace
    The little clouds go by.

Yet the back yards are bare and brown
    With only one unchanging tree—
I could not be so sure of Spring
    Save that it sings in me.

April Rain Song

Langston Hughes
1902–1967

Let the rain kiss you.
Let the rain beat upon your head with silver
  liquid drops.
Let the rain sing you a lullaby.
The rain makes still pools on the sidewalk.
The rain makes running pools in the gutter.
The rain plays a little sleep-song on our roof
  at night—

And I love the rain.

Rain

James Whitcomb Riley
1849–1916

It ain't no use to grumble and complain;
  It's jest as cheap and easy to rejoice;
When God sorts out the weather and sends
    rain,
  Why, rain's my choice.

Mud

Polly Chase Boyden

Mud is very nice to feel
    All squishy-squash between the toes!
I'd rather wade in wiggly mud
    Than smell a yellow rose.

From *"The Cloud"*

Percy Bysshe Shelley
1792–1822

I bring fresh showers for the thirsting
    flowers,
  From the seas and the streams;
I bear light shade for the leaves when laid
  In their noonday dreams.
From my wings are shaken the dews that
    waken
  The sweet buds every one,
When rocked to rest on their mother's
    breast,
  As she dances about the sun.
I wield the flail of the lashing hail,
  And whiten the green plains under;
And then again I dissolve it in rain,
  And laugh as I pass in thunder.

A Brilliant Day

Charles Turner
1808–1879

O keen pellucid air! nothing can lurk
Or disavow itself on this bright day;
The small rain-plashes shine from far away,
The tiny emmet glitters at his work;
The bee looks blithe and gay, and as she
    plies
Her task, and moves and sidles round the
    cup
Of this spring flower, to drink its honey up,
Her glassy wings, like oars that dip and rise,
Gleam momently. Pure-bosom'd, clear of
    fog,
The long lake glistens, while the glorious
    beam
Bespangles the wet joints and floating leaves
Of water-plants, whose every point receives
His light; and jellies of the spawning frog,
Unmark'd before, like piles of jewels seem!

May Morning

Celia Thaxter
1835–1894

Warm, wild, rainy wind, blowing fitfully,
Stirring dreamy breakers on the slumberous
  May sea,
What shall fail to answer thee? What thing
  shall withstand
The spell of thine enchantment, flowing over
  sea and land?

All along the swamp-edge in the rain I go;
All about my head thou the loosened locks
  dost blow;
Like the German goose-girl in the fairy tale,
I watch across the shining pool my flock of
  ducks that sail.

Redly gleam the rose-haws, dripping with the
  wet,
Fruit of sober autumn, glowing crimson yet;
Slender swords of iris leaves cut the water
  clear,
And light green creeps the tender grass,
  thick-spreading far and near.

27

Every last year's stalk is set with brown or
  golden studs;
All the boughs of bayberry are thick with
  scented buds;
Islanded in turfy velvet, where the ferns
  uncurl,
Lo! the large white duck's egg glimmers like
  a pearl!

Softly sing the billows, rushing, whispering
  low;
Freshly, oh, deliciously, the warm, wild wind
  doth blow!
Plaintive bleat of new-washed lambs comes
  faint from far away;
And clearly cry the little birds, alert and
  blithe and gay.

O happy, happy morning! O dear, familiar
  place!
O warm, sweet tears of Heaven, fast falling
  on my face!
O well-remembered, rainy wind, blow all my
  care away,
That I may be a child again this blissful
  morn of May.

The Seed Shop

Muriel Stuart
1912–

Here in a quiet and dusty room they lie,
Faded as crumbled stone or shifting sand,
Forlorn as ashes, shriveled, scentless, dry—
Meadows and gardens running through my
    hand.

In this brown husk a dale of hawthorn
    dreams;
A cedar in this narrow cell is thrust
That will drink deeply of a century's
    streams;
These lilies shall make summer on my dust.

Here in their safe and simple house of death,
Sealed in their shells, a million roses leap;
Here I can blow a garden with my breath,
And in my hand a forest lies asleep.

The Gardener

Arthur Symons
1865–1945

The gardener in his old brown hands
Turns over the brown earth,
As if he loves and understands
The flowers before their birth,
The fragile little childish strands
He buries in the earth.
Like pious children one by one
He sets them head by head,
And draws the clothes, when all is done,
Closely about each head,
And leaves his children to sleep on
In the one quiet bed.

Page from a Journal

Hermann Hesse
1877–1962

On the slope behind the house today
I cut through roots and rocks and
Dug a hole, deep and wide,
Carted away from it each stone
And all the friable, thin earth.
Then I knelt there a moment, walked
In the old woods, bent down again, using
A trowel and both my hands to scoop
Black, decaying woods-soil with the warm
Smell of fungi from the trunk of a rotting
Chestnut tree—two heavy buckets full I
　　carried
Back to the hole and planted the tree inside;
Carefully I covered the roots with peaty soil,
Slowly poured sun-warmed water over them,
Mudding them gently until the soil settled.
It stands there, young and small,
Will go on standing when we are gone
And the huge uproar, endless urgency and
Fearful delirium of our days forgotten.

The föhn will bend it, rainstorms tear at it,
The sun will laugh, wet snow weigh it down,
The siskin and the nuthatch make it their
     home,
And the silent hedgehog burrow at its foot.
All it has ever experienced, tasted, suffered:
The course of years, generations of animals,
Oppression, recovery, friendship of sun and
     wind
Will pour forth each day in the song
Of its rustling foliage, in the friendly
Gesture of its gently swaying crown,
In the delicate sweet scent of resinous
Sap moistening the sleep-glued buds,
And the eternal game of lights and
Shadows it plays with itself, content.

Planting Trees

V. H. Friedlaender

Today six slender fruit trees stand
Where yesterday were none;
They have been planted by my hand,
And they shall dazzle in the sun
When all my springs are done.

Two apples shall unfold their rose,
Two cherries their snow, two pears;
And fruit shall hang where blossom blows,
When I am gone from these sweet airs
To where none knows or cares.

My heart is glad, my heart is high
With sudden ecstasy;
I have given back, before I die,
Some thanks for every lovely tree
That dead men grew for me.

From *"The Planting of the Apple-Tree"*

William Cullen Bryant
1794–1878

Come, let us plant the apple-tree.
Cleave the tough greensward with the spade;
Wide let its hollow bed be made;
There gently lay the roots, and there
Sift the dark mould with kindly care,
　And press it o'er them tenderly,
As round the sleeping infant's feet
We softly fold the cradle-sheet;
　So plant we the apple-tree.

　What plant we in this apple-tree?
Buds, which the breath of summer days
Shall lengthen into leafy sprays;
Boughs where the thrush with crimson
　breast
Shall haunt, and sing, and hide her nest;
　We plant, upon the sunny lea,
A shadow for the noontide hour,
A shelter from a summer shower,
　When we plant the apple-tree.

What plant we in this apple-tree?
Sweets for a hundred flowery springs
To load the May-wind's restless wings,
When, from the orchard row, he pours
Its fragrance through our open doors;
    A world of blossoms for the bee,
Flowers for the sick girl's silent room
For the glad infant sprigs of bloom,
    We plant with the apple-tree.

What plant we in this apple-tree!
Fruits that shall swell in sunny June,
And redden in the August noon,
And drop, when gentle airs come by,
That fan the blue September sky,
    While children come, with cries of glee,
And seek them where the fragrant grass
Betrays their bed to those who pass,
    At the foot of the apple-tree.

And when, above this apple-tree,
The winter stars are quivering bright,
And winds go howling through the night,
Girls, whose young eyes o'erflow with mirth,
Shall peel its fruit by cottage hearth,
    And guests in prouder homes shall see,
Heaped with the grape of Cintra's vine
    And golden orange of the Line,
    The fruit of the apple-tree.

The fruitage of the apple-tree
Winds and our flag of stripe and star
Shall bear to coasts that lie afar,
Where men shall wonder at the view,
And ask in what fair groves they grew;
And sojourners beyond the sea
Shall think of childhood's careless day
And long, long hours of summer play,
In the shade of the apple-tree.

Oh, Fair to See

Christina Rossetti
1830–1894

Oh, fair to see
Bloom-laden cherry tree,
　Arrayed in sunny white:
　An April day's delight,
Oh, fair to see!

Oh, fair to see
Fruit-laden cherry tree,
　With balls of shining red
　Decking a leafy head,
Oh, fair to see!

Pruning

John Philips
1676–1709

Let the arched knife
Well sharpen'd now assail the spreading
  shades
Of vegetables, and their thirsty limbs
Dissever: for the genial moisture, due
To apples, otherwise mispends itself
In barren twigs, and for th'expected crop,
Nought but vain shoots, and empty leaves
  abound.
  When swelling buds their odorous foliage
  shed,
And gently harden into fruit, the wise
Spare not the little offsprings, if they grow
Redundant; but the thronging clusters thin
By kind avulsion: else the starveling brood,
Void of sufficient sustenance, will yield
A slender autumn; which the niggard soul
Too late shall weep, and curse his thrifty
  hand,
That would not timely ease the ponderous
  boughs.

From *"The Ploughman"*

Oliver Wendell Holmes
1809–1894

First in the field before the reddening sun,
Last in the shadows when the day is done,
Line after line, along the bursting sod,
Marks the broad acres where his feet have
  trod.
Still where he treads the stubborn clods
  divide,
The smooth fresh furrow opens deep and
  wide;
Matted and dense the tangled turf upheaves,
Mellow and dark the ridgy cornfield cleaves;
Up the steep hillside, where the laboring
  train
Slants the long track that scores the level
  plain,
Through the moist valley, clogged with
  oozing clay,
The patient convoy breaks its destined way;
At every turn the loosening chains resound,
The swinging ploughshare circles glistening
  round,

Till the wide field one billowy waste appears,
And wearied hands unbind the panting
  steers.

These are the hands whose sturdy labor
  brings
The peasant's food, the golden pomp of
  kings;
This is the page whose letters shall be seen,
Changed by the sun to words of living green;
This is the scholar whose immortal pen
Spells the first lesson hunger taught to men;
These are the lines that heaven-commanded
  Toil
Shows on his deed,—the charter of the soil!

Planting Flowers on the Eastern Embankment

Written while Governor of Chung-Chou

Po Chü-I
772–846

I took money and bought flowering trees
And planted them out on the bank to the
    east of the keep.
I simply bought whatever had most blooms,
Not caring whether peach, apricot, or plum.
A hundred fruits, all mixed up together;
A thousand branches, flowering in due
    rotation.
Each has its season coming early or late;
But to all alike the fertile soil is kind.
The red flowers hang like a heavy mist;
The white flowers gleam like a fall of snow.
The wandering bees cannot bear to leave
    them;
The sweet birds also come there to roost.
In front there flows an ever-running stream;
Beneath there is built a little flat terrace.

Sometimes I sweep the flagstones of the
    terrace;
Sometimes, in the wind, I raise my cup and
    drink.
The flower branches screen my head from
    the sun;
The flower buds fall down into my lap.
Alone drinking, alone singing my songs
I do not notice that the moon is level with
    the steps.
The people of Pa do not care for flowers;
All the spring no one has come to look.
But their Governor General, alone with his
    cup of wine
Sits till evening and will not move from the
    place!

Translated by Arthur Waley

A Contemplation upon Flowers

Henry King
1592–1669

Brave flowers, that I could gallant it like you
   And be as little vain!
You come abroad, and make a harmless
     show,
   And to your beds of earth again;
You are not proud, you know your birth,
For your embroidered garments are from
     earth.

You do obey your months, and times, but I
   Would have it ever spring;
My fate would know no winter, never die,
   Nor think of such a thing.
Oh that I could my bed of earth but view,
And smile, and look as cheerfully as you!

Oh teach me to see death, and not to fear,
   But rather to take truce;
How often have I seen you at a bier,
   And there look fresh and spruce.
You fragrant flowers then teach me that my
   breath
Like yours may sweeten and perfume my
   death.

The Use of Flowers

Mary Howitt
1799–1888

God might have bade the earth bring forth
  Enough for great and small,
The oak-tree and the cedar-tree,
  Without a flower at all.
We might have had enough, enough
  For every want of ours,
For luxury, medicine, and toil,
  And yet have had no flowers.

Then wherefore, wherefore were they made,
  All dyed with rainbow light,
All fashioned with supremest grace,
  Upspringing day and night:—
Springing in valleys green and low,
  And on the mountains high,
And in the silent wilderness
  Where no man passes by?

Our outward life requires them not,—
  Then wherefore had they birth?—
To minister delight to man,
  To beautify the earth;
To comfort man,—to whisper hope,
  Whene'er his faith is dim,
For who so careth for the flowers
  Will care much more for him!

The Life of Flowers

Walter Savage Landor
1775–1864

When hath wind or rain
Borne hard upon weak plant that wanted me,
And I (however they might bluster round)
Walkt off? 'T were most ungrateful; for
    sweet scents
Are the swift vehicles of still sweeter
    thoughts,
And nurse and pillow the dull memory
That would let drop without them her best
    stores.
They bring me tales of youth and tones of
    love,
And 't is and ever was my wish and way
To let all flowers live freely, and all die
(Whene'er their Genius bids their souls
    depart)
Among their kindred in their native place.
I never pluck the rose; the violet's head

Hath shaken with my breath upon its bank
And not reproacht me; the ever-sacred cup
Of the pure lily hath between my hands
Felt safe, unsoiled, nor lost one grain of
    gold.

To Blossoms

Robert Herrick
1591–1674

Fair pledges of a fruitful tree,
　　Why do ye fall so fast?
　　Your date is not so past
But you may stay yet here awhile
　　To blush and gently smile,
　　　　And go at last.

What! were ye born to be
　　An hour or half's delight,
　　And so to bid good-night?
'T is pity Nature brought ye forth,
　　Merely to show your worth,
　　　　And lose you quite.

But you are lovely leaves, where we
　　May read how soon things have
　　Their end, though ne'er so brave;
And after they have shown their pride
　　Like you awhile, they glide
　　　　Into the grave.

Flowers

Thomas Hood
1799–1845

I will not have the mad Clytie,
   Whose head is turned by the sun;
The tulip is a courtly quean,
   Whom, therefore, I will shun:
The cowslip is a country wench,
   The violet is a nun;—
But I will woo the dainty rose,
   The queen of every one.

The pea is but a wanton witch,
   In too much haste to wed,
And clasps her rings on every hand;
   The wolfsbane I should dread;
Nor will I dreary rosemarye,
   That always mourns the dead;
But I will woo the dainty rose,
   With her cheeks of tender red.

The lily is all in white, like a saint,
  And so is no mate for me;
And the daisy's cheek is tipped with a blush
  She is of such low degree;
Jasmine is sweet, and has many loves,
  And the broom's betrothed to the bee;—
But I will plight with the dainty rose,
  For fairest of all is she.

The First Dandelion

Walt Whitman
1819–1892

Simple and fresh and fair from winter's close
    emerging,
As if no artifice of fashion, business,
    politics, has ever been,
Forth from its sunny nook of shelter'd
    grass—innocent, golden, calm as the
    dawn,
The spring's first dandelion shows its trustful
    face.

Dandelions

John Albee
1833–1915

Now dandelions in the short, new grass,
Through all their rapid stages daily pass;
No bee yet visits them; each has its place,
Still near enough to see the other's face.
Unkenn'd the bud, so like the grass and
    ground
In our old country yards where thickest
    found;
Some morn it opes a little golden sun,
And sets in its own west when day is done.
In few days more't is old and silvery gray,
And though so close to earth it made its
    stay,
Lo! now it findeth wings and lightly flies,
A spirit form, till on the sight it dies.

From *"To the Dandelion"*

James Russell Lowell
1819–1891

Dear common flower, that grow'st beside
    the way,
Fringing the dusty road with harmless gold,
    First pledge of blithesome May,
Which children pluck, and, full of pride,
    uphold,
    High-hearted buccaneers, o'erjoyed that
    they
An Eldorado in the grass have found,
Which not the rich earth's ample round
    May match in wealth, thou art more dear
    to me
    Than all the prouder summer blooms may
    be.

My childhood's earliest thoughts are
    linked with thee;
The sight of thee calls back the robin's song,
    Who, from the dark old tree
Beside the door, sang clearly all day long,
    And I, secure in childish piety,

Listened as if I heard an angel sing
With news from heaven, which he could
    bring
  Fresh every day to my untainted ears
  When birds and flowers and I were happy
    peers.

Yellow Jessamine

Constance Fenimore Woolson
1840–1894

In tangled wreaths, in clustered gleaming
    stars,
  In floating, curling sprays,
The golden flower comes shining through the
    woods
  These February days;
Forth go all hearts, all hands, from out the
    town,
  To bring her gayly in,
This wild, sweet Princess of far Florida—
  The yellow jessamine.

The live-oaks smile to see her lovely face
  Peep from the thickets; shy,
She hides behind the leaves her golden buds
  Till, bolder grown, on high
She curls a tendril, throws a spray, then
    flings
  Herself aloft in glee,
And, bursting into thousand blossoms,
    swings
  In wreaths from tree to tree.

The dwarf-palmetto on his knees adores
　　This Princess of the air;
The lone pine-barren broods afar and sighs,
　　"Ah! come, lest I despair";
The myrtle-thickets and ill-tempered thorns
　　Quiver and thrill within,
As through their leaves they feel the dainty
　　　　touch
　　Of yellow jessamine.

The garden-roses wonder as they see
　　The wreaths of golden bloom,
Brought in from the far woods with eager
　　　　haste
　　To deck the poorest room,
The rich man's house, alike; the loaded
　　　　hands
　　Give sprays to all they meet,
Till, gay with flowers, the people come and
　　　　go,
　　And all the air is sweet.

The Southern land, well weary of its green
    Which may not fall nor fade,
Bestirs itself to greet the lovely flower
    With leaves of fresher shade;
The pine has tassles, and the orange-trees
    Their fragrant work begin:
The spring has come—has come to Florida,
    With yellow jessamine.

Daffodils

William Wordsworth
1770–1850

I wandered lonely as a cloud
    That floats on high o'er vales and hills,
When all at once I saw a crowd,
    A host, of golden daffodils;
Beside the lake, beneath the trees,
Fluttering and dancing in the breeze.

Continuous as the stars that shine
    And twinkle on the Milky Way,
They stretched in never-ending line
    Along the margin of a bay:
Ten thousand saw I at a glance,
Tossing their heads in sprightly dance.

The waves beside them danced, but they
    Out-did the sparkling waves in glee:
A poet could not but be gay,
    In such a jocund company:
I gazed—and gazed—but little thought
What wealth the show to me had brought:

For oft, when on my couch I lie
In vacant or in pensive mood,
They flash upon that inward eye
Which is the bliss of solitude;
And then my heart with pleasure fills,
And dances with the daffodils.

To Daffodils

Robert Herrick
1591–1674

Faire daffadills, we weep to see
  You haste away so soone;
As yet the early-rising sun
  Has not attained his noone.
      Stay, stay,
  Until the hastening day
      Has run
  But to the even-song;
And having prayed together, we
  Will goe with you along.

We have short time to stay as you,
  We have as short a spring;
As quick a growth, to meet decay,
  As you or anything.
      We die,
  As your hours doe, and drie
      Away,
  Like to the summer's raine,
Or as the pearles of morning's dew,
  Ne'er to be found againe.

White Azaleas

Harriet McEwen Kimball
1834–?

Azalea—whitest of white!
  White as the drifted snow
Fresh-fallen out of the night,
  Before the coming glow
Tinges the morning light;
  When the light is like the snow,
      White,
And the silence is like the light:
  Light, and silence, and snow,—
      All—white!
White! not a hint
Of the creamy tint
      A rose will hold,
      The whitest rose, in its inmost fold;
Not a possible blush;
White as an embodied hush;
  A very rapture of white;
A wedlock of silence and light:
White, white as the wonder undefiled
Of Eve just wakened in Paradise;
Nay, white as the angel of a child
  That looks into God's own eyes!

Pink, Small and Punctual
(Arbutus)

Emily Dickinson
1830–1886

Pink, small and punctual,
Aromatic, low,
Covert in April,
Candid in May,

Dear to the moss,
Known by the knoll,
Next to the robin
In every human soul.

Bold little beauty,
Bedecked with thee,
Nature forswears
Antiquity.

Iris

William Carlos Williams
1883–1963

a burst of iris so that
come down for
breakfast

we searched through the
rooms for
that

sweetest odor and at
first could not
find its

source then a blue as
of the sea
struck

startling us from among
those trumpeting
petals

To a Lily

James Matthew Legare
1823–1859

Go bow thy head in gentle spite,
Thou lily white,
For she who spies thee waving here,
With thee in beauty can compare
As day with night.

Soft are thy leaves and white: her arms
Boast whiter charms.
Thy stem prone bent with loveliness
Of maiden grace possesseth less:
Therein she charms.

Thou in thy lake dost see
Thyself: so she
Beholds her image in her eyes
Reflected. Thus did Venus rise
From out the sea.

Inconsolate, bloom not again.
Thou rival vain
Of her whose charms have thine outdone,
Whose purity might spot the sun,
And make thy leaf a stain.

Violets

John Moultrie
1799–1874

Under the green hedges, after the snow,
There do the dear little violets grow;
Hiding their modest and beautiful heads
Under the hawthorn in soft mossy beds.

Sweet as the roses and blue as the sky,
Down there do the dear little violets lie;
Hiding their heads where they scarce may be
    seen,
By the leaves you may know where the violet
    hath been.

To Violets

Robert Herrick
1591–1674

Welcome Maids of Honour,
   You do bring
   In the Spring;
And wait upon her.

She has virgins many,
   Fresh and fair;
   Yet you are
More sweet than any.

Y'are the maiden posies,
   And so grac'd,
   To be plac'd,
'Fore damask roses.

Yet though thus respected,
   By and by
   Ye do lie
Poor girls, neglected.

The Yellow Violet

William Cullen Bryant
1794–1878

When beechen buds begin to swell,
　　And woods the blue-bird's warble know,
The yellow violet's modest bell
　　Peeps from the last year's leaves below.

Ere russet fields their green resume,
　　Sweet flower, I love, in forest bare,
To meet thee, when thy faint perfume
　　Alone is in the virgin air.

Of all her train, the hands of Spring
　　First plant thee in the watery mould,
And I have seen thee blossoming
　　Beside the snow-bank's edges cold.

Thy parent sun, who bade thee view
　　Pale skies, and chilling moisture sip,
Has bathed thee in his own bright hue,
　　And streaked with jet thy glowing lip.

Yet slight thy form, and low thy seat,
    And earthward bent thy gentle eye,
Unapt the passing view to meet,
    When loftier flowers are flaunting nigh.

Oft, in the sunless April day,
    Thy early smile has stayed my walk;
But midst the gorgeous blooms of May,
    I passed thee on thy humble stalk.

So they, who climb to wealth, forget
    The friends in darker fortunes tried.
I copied them—but I regret
    That I should ape the ways of pride.

And when again the genial hour
    Awakes the painted tribes of light,
I'll not o'erlook the modest flower
    That made the woods of April bright.

Red Geranium
and Godly Mignonette

D. H. Lawrence
1885–1930

Imagine that any mind ever *thought* a red
geranium!
As if the redness of a red geranium could be
anything but a sensual experience,
and as if sensual experience could take place
before there were any senses.
We know that even God could not imagine
the redness of a red geranium
nor the smell of mignonette
when geraniums were not, and mignonette
neither.
And even when they were, even God would
have to have a nose
to smell at the mignonette.
You can't imagine the Holy Ghost sniffing
at cherry-pie heliotrope.
Or the Most High, during the coal age,
cudgelling his mighty brains
even if he had any brains: straining his
mighty mind

to think, among the moss and mud of lizards
    and mastodons
to think out, in the abstract, when all was
    twilit green and muddy:
"Now there shall be tum-tiddly-um, and
    tum-tiddly-um,
hey-presto! scarlet geranium!"

We know it couldn't be done.
But imagine, among the mud and mastodons
god sighing and yearning with tremendous
    creative yearning, in that dark green mess
oh, for some other beauty, some other beauty
that blossomed at last, red geranium, and
    mignonette.

Red Geraniums

Martha Haskell Clark
1885–?

Life did not bring me silken gowns,
Nor jewels for my hair,
Nor signs of gabled foreign towns
In distant countries fair,
But I can glimpse, beyond my pane, a green
and friendly hill,
And red geraniums aflame upon my window
sill.

The brambled cares of everyday,
The tiny humdrum things,
May bind my feet when they would stray,
But still my heart had wings
While red geraniums are bloomed against my
window glass,
And low above my green-sweet hill the gypsy
wind-clouds pass.

And if my dreamings ne'er come true,
The brightest and the best,
But leave me lone my journey through,
I'll set my heart at rest,
And thank God for home-sweet things, a
  green and friendly hill,
And red geraniums aflame upon my window
  sill.

Marigolds

Louise Driscoll
1875–1957

Do you like marigolds?
 If you do
Then my garden is
 Gay for you!

I've been cutting their
 Fragrant stalks
Where they lean on
 The garden walks.

The head's too heavy for
 The brittle stem,
A careless touch and
 You've broken them.

Each one shines like a
 Separate star
Set in some heaven where
 Gardens are.

My hands smell of the
  Herb-like scent,
Telling what garden
  Way I went.

Pungent, vivid and
  Strong, they stay
Long after Summer has
  Gone away.

Do you like marigolds?
  Here's a pledge
To meet the frost with
  A golden edge—

To go as far as
  A weak thing may
Linking to-morrow with
  Yesterday.

Poppies

P. A. Ropes

The strange, bright dancers
Are in the garden.
The wind of summer
Is a soft music.
Scarlet and orange,
Flaming and golden,
The strange, bright dancers
Move to the music.
And some are whiter
Than snow in winter,
And float like snowflakes
Drifting the garden.
Oh, have you seen them,
The strange, bright dancers,
Nodding and swaying
To the wind's music?

The Broom Flower

Mary Howitt
1799–1888

Oh the Broom, the yellow Broom,
   The ancient poet sung it,
And dear it is on summer days
   To lie at rest among it.

I know the realms where people say
   The flowers have not their fellow;
I know where they shine out like suns,
   The crimson and the yellow.

I know where ladies live enchained
   In luxury's silken fetters,
And flowers as bright as glittering gems
   Are used for written letters.

But ne'er was flower so fair as this,
   In modern days or olden;
It groweth on its nodding stem
   Like to a garland golden.

And all about my mother's door
    Shine out its glittering bushes,
And down the glen, where clear as light
    The mountain-water gushes.

Take all the rest; but give me this,
    And the bird that nestles in it;
I love it, for it loves the Broom—
    The green and yellow linnet.

Well call the rose the queen of flowers,
    And boast of that of Sharon,
Of lilies like to marble cups,
    And the golden rod of Aaron:

I care not how these flowers may be
    Beloved of man and woman;
The Broom is the flower for me,
    That groweth on the common.

Oh the Broom, the yellow Broom,
    The ancient poet sung it,
And dear it is on summer days
    To lie at rest among it.

The Morning-Glory

Florence Earle Coates
1850–1927

Was it worth while to paint so fair
    Thy every leaf—to vein with faultless art
Each petal, taking the boon light and air
    Of summer so to heart?

To bring thy beauty unto perfect flower,
    Then, like a passing fragrance or a smile,
Vanish away, beyond recovery's power—
    Was it, frail bloom, worth while?

Thy silence answers: "Life was mine!
    And I, who pass without regret or grief,
Have cared the more to make my moment
    fine,
    Because it was so brief.

"In its first radiance I have seen
    The sun!—why tarry then till comes the
    night?
I go my way, content that I have been
    Part of the morning light!"

Fringed Gentians

Amy Lowell
1874–1925

Near where I live there is a lake
As blue as blue can be; winds make
It dance as they go blowing by.
I think it curtsies to the sky.

It's just a lake of lovely flowers,
And my Mamma says they are ours;
But they are not like those we grow
To be our very own, you know.

We have a splendid garden, there
Are lots of flowers everywhere;
Roses, and pinks, and four-o'clocks,
And hollyhocks, and evening stocks.

Mamma lets us pick them, but never
Must we pick any gentians—ever!
For if we carried them away
They'd die of homesickness that day.

To the Daisy

William Wordsworth
1770–1850

With little here to do or see
Of things that in the great world be,
Sweet Daisy! oft I talk to thee
        For thou art worthy,
Thou unassuming Commonplace
Of Nature, with that homely face,
And yet with something of a grace
        Which love makes for thee!

Oft on the dappled turf at ease
I sit and play with similes
Loose types of things through all degrees,
        Thoughts of thy raising;
And many a fond and idle name
I give to thee, for praise or blame
As is the humour of the game,
        While I am gazing.

A nun demure, of lowly port;
Or sprightly maiden, of Love's court,
In thy simplicity the sport
        Of all temptations;

A queen in crown of rubies drest;
A starveling in a scanty vest;
Are all, as seems to suit thee best,
    Thy appellations.
A little Cyclops, with one eye
Staring to threaten and defy,
That thought comes next—and instantly
    The freak is over.
The shape will vanish, and behold!
A silver shield with boss of gold
That spreads itself, some fairy bold
    In fight to cover.

I see thee glittering from afar—
And then thou art a pretty star,
Not quite so fair as many are
    In heaven above thee!
Yet like a star, with glittering crest,
Self-poised in air thou seem'st to rest;—
May peace come never to his nest
    Who shall reprove thee!

Sweet Flower! for by that name at last
When all my reveries are past
I call thee, and to that cleave fast,
    Sweet silent Creature!
That breath'st with me in sun and air,
Do thou, as thou art wont, repair
My heart with gladness, and a share
    Of thy meek nature!

Buttercups and Daisies

Mary Howitt
1799–1888

Buttercups and daisies
　　Oh, the pretty flowers;
Coming ere the spring-time,
　　To tell of sunny hours,
While the trees are leafless,
　　While the fields are bare,
Buttercups and daisies
　　Spring up here and there.

Ere the snowdrop peepeth,
　　Ere the crocus bold,
Ere the early primrose
　　Opes its paly gold—
Somewhere on the sunny bank
　　Buttercups are bright;
Somewhere 'mong the frozen grass
　　Peeps the daisy white.

Sunflower

John Updike
1932–

Sunflower, of flowers
the most lonely,
yardstick of hours,
long-term stander
in empty spaces,
shunner of bowers,
indolent bender
seldom, in only
the sharpest of showers:
tell us, why
is it your face is a snarl of jet swirls
and golden arrows, a burning
old lion face high
in a cornflower sky,
yet by turning
your head, we find
you wear a girl's
bonnet behind?

Ah, Sunflower

William Blake
1757–1827

Ah, Sunflower! weary of time,
Who countest the steps of the Sun;
Seeking after that sweet golden clime,
Where the traveler's journey is done;

Where the Youth pined away with desire,
And the pale Virgin shrouded in snow,
Arise from their graves, and aspire
Where my Sunflower wishes to go!

Hyacinths to Feed Thy Soul

Attributed to the Gulistan of
Moslih Eddin Saadi
1184–1291

If of thy mortal goods thou art bereft,
And from thy slender store two loaves alone
   to thee are left,
Sell one, and with the dole
Buy hyacinths to feed thy soul.

Die Lotosblume Ängstigt

Heinrich Heine
1797–1856

The Lotus-flower doth languish
  Beneath the sun's fierce light;
With drooping head she waiteth
  All dreamily for night.

The Moon is her true lover,
  He wakes her with his glance:
To him she unveils gladly
  Her gentle countenance.

She blooms and glows and brightens,
  Intent on him above;
Exhaling, weeping, trembling
  With ever-yearning love.

Translated by James Thomson

The Rhodora

On Being Asked,
Whence Is the Flower?

Ralph Waldo Emerson
1803–1882

In May, when sea-winds pierced our
    solitudes,
I found the fresh Rhodora in the woods,
Spreading its leafless blooms in a damp
    nook,
To please the desert and the sluggish brook.
The purple petals, fallen in the pool,
Made the black water with their beauty gay;
Here might the red-bird come his plumes to
    cool,
And court the flower that cheapens his array.
Rhodora! if the sages ask thee why
This charm is wasted on the earth and sky,
Tell them, dear, that if eyes were made for
    seeing,
Then Beauty is its own excuse for being:

Why thou wert there, O rival of the rose!
I never thought to ask, I never knew:
But, in my simple ignorance, suppose
The self-same Power that brought me there
    brought you.

Idyll of the Rose

Decimus Magnus Ausonius
310–395

'Twas spring, and dawn returning breathed
  new-born
From saffron skies the bracing chill of
  morn.
Before day's orient chargers went a breeze,
That whispered: Rise, the sweets of morning
  seize!
In watered gardens where the cross-paths
  ran,
Freshness and health I sought ere noon
  began:
I watched from bending grasses how the rime
In clusters hung, or gemmed the beds of
  thyme;
How the round beads, on herb and leaf
  outspread,
Rolled with the weight of dews from heaven's
  bright shed.
Saw the rose-gardens in their Paestan bloom
Hoar 'neath the dawn-star rising through the
  gloom.

On every bush those separate splendors
    gleam,
Doomed to be quenched by day's first arrowy
    beam.
Here might one doubt: doth morn from roses
    steal
Their redness, or the rose with dawn anneal?
One hue, one dew, one morn makes both
    serene;
Of star and flower one Venus reigns the
    queen.
Perchance one scent have they: the star's
    o'erhead
Far, far exhales, the flower's at hand is shed.
Goddess of star, goddess of rose no less,
The Paphian flings o'er both her crimson
    dress.
Now had the moment passed wherein the
    brood
Of clustering buds seemed one twin
    sisterhood.
This flower, enlaced with leaves, shows
    naught but green;
That shoots a roseate streak from forth the
    screen:
One opes her pyramid and purple spire,
Emerging into plenitude of fire:
Another thrusts her verdant veil aside,
Counting her petals one by one with pride:

Expands her radiant cup of gorgeous hues,
And brings dense hidden veins of gold to
    view:
She who had burned erewhile, a flower of
    flame,
Now pales and droops her fainting head with
    shame:—
So that I mused how swift time steals all
    worth,
How roses age and wither with their birth;
Yea, while I speak, the flower with crimson
    crowned
Hath fallen and shed her glories on the
    ground.
So many births, forms, fates with changes
    fraught,
One day begins and one day brings to
    naught!
Grieve we that flowers should have so short a
    grace,
That Nature shows and steals her gifts
    apace?
Long as the day, so long the red rose lasts;
Eld following close on youth her beauty
    blasts:
That flower which Phosphor newly-born had
    known,
Hesper returning finds a wrinkled crone:

Yet well if, though some brief days past she
    die,
Her life be lengthened through posterity!
Pluck roses, girl, when flower, when youth is
    new,
Mindful the while that thus time flies for
    you.

Translated by John Addington Symonds

Roses

George Eliot
1819–1880

You love the roses—so do I. I wish
The sky would rain down roses, as they rain
From off the shaken bush. Why will it not?
Then all the valley would be pink and white
And soft to tread on. They would fall as
    light
As feathers, smelling sweet: and it would be
Like sleeping and yet waking, all at once.

Rose and Root

A Fable of Two Lives

John James Piatt
1835–1917

The Rose aloft in sunny air,
    Beloved alike by bird and bee,
Takes for the dark Root little care
    That toils below it ceaselessly.

I put my question to the flower:
    "Pride of the Summer, garden queen,
Why livest thou thy little hour?"
    And the Rose answered, "I am seen."

I put my question to the Root,
    "I mine the earth content," it said,
"A hidden miner underfoot:
    I know a Rose is overhead."

Said the Rose

George H. Miles
1824–1871

I am weary of the Garden,
    Said the Rose;
For the winter winds are sighing,
All my playmates round me dying,
And my leaves will soon be lying
    'Neath the snows.

But I hear my Mistress coming,
    Said the Rose;
She will take me to her chamber,
Where the honeysuckles clamber,
And I'll bloom there all December
    Spite the snows.

Sweeter fell her lily finger
    Than the bee!
Ah, how feebly I resisted,
Smoothed my thorns, and e'en assisted
As all blushing I was twisted
    Off my tree.

And fixed me in her bosom
    Like a star;
And I flashed there all the morning,
Jasmin, honeysuckle scorning,
Parasites forever fawning
    That they are.

And when evening came she set me
    In a vase
All of rare and radiant metal,
And I felt her red lips settle
On my leaves till each proud petal
    Touched her face.

And I shone about her slumbers
    Like a light;
And, I said, instead of weeping,
In the garden vigil keeping,
Here I'll watch my Mistress sleeping
    Every night.

But when morning with its sunbeams
    Softly shone,
In the mirror where she braided
Her brown hair I saw how jaded,
Old and colorless and faded,
    I had grown.

Not a drop of dew was on me,
    Never one;
From my leaves no odors started,
All my perfume had departed,
I lay pale and broken-hearted
    In the sun.

Still I said, her smile is better
    Than the rain;
Though my fragrance may forsake me,
To her bosom she will take me,
And with crimson kisses make me
    Young again.

So she took me . . . gazed a second . . .
    Half a sigh . . .
Then, alas, can hearts so harden?
Without ever asking pardon,
Threw me back into the garden,
    There to die.

How the jealous garden gloried
    In my fall!
How the honeysuckle chid me,
How the sneering jasmins bid me
Light the long gray grass that hid me
    Like a pall.

There I lay beneath her window
 In a swoon,
Till the earthworm o'er me trailing
Woke me just at twilight's failing,
As the whip-poor-will was wailing
 To the moon.

But I hear the storm-winds stirring
 In their lair;
And I know they soon will lift me
In their giant arms and sift me
Into ashes as they drift me
 Through the air.

So I pray them in their mercy
 Just to take
From my heart of hearts, or near it,
The last living leaf, and bear it
To her feet, and bid her wear it
 For my sake.

My Garden

W. H. Davies
1871–1940

The lilac in my garden comes to bloom,
    The apple, plum and cherry wait their
      hour,
The honeysuckle climbs from pole to pole—
    And the rockery has a stone that's now a
      flower,
Jeweled by moss in every tiny hole!

Close to my lilac there's a small bird's nest
    Of quiet, young, half-sleeping birds: but
      when
I look, each little rascal—five I've
      reckoned—
    Opens a mouth so large and greedy then,
He swallows his own face in half a second!

A Garden Song

Austin Dobson
1840–1921

Here in this sequestered close
Bloom the hyacinth and rose,
Here beside the modest stock
Flaunts the flaring hollyhock;
Here, without a pang, one sees
Ranks, conditions and degrees.

All the seasons run their race
In this quiet resting place;
Peach and apricot and fig
Here will ripen and grow big;
Here is store and overplus,—
More had not Alcinoüs!

Here, in alleys cool and green,
Far ahead the thrush is seen;
Here along the southern wall
Keeps the bee his festival;
All is quiet else—afar
Sounds of toil and turmoil are.

Here be shadows large and long;
Here be spaces meet for song;
Grant, O garden-god, that I,
Now that none profane is nigh,—
Now that mood and moment please,—
Find the fair Pierides!

In Green Old Gardens

Violet Fane
1843–1905

In green old gardens, hidden away
   From sight of revel and sound of strife,
      Where the bird may sing out his soul
      ere he die,
Nor fears for the night, so he lives his day;
Where the high red walls, which are growing
   gray
      With their lichen and moss
      embroideries,
   Seem sadly and sternly to shut out life,
Because it is often as red as they;

Where even the bee has time to glide
   (Gathering gayly his honey's store)
      Right to the heart of the old-world
      flowers—
China-asters and purple stocks,
Dahlias and tall red hollyhocks,
      Laburnums raining their golden
      showers,

Columbines prim of the folded core,
And lupins, and larkspurs, and "London
  pride";

Where the heron is waiting amongst the
  reeds,
  Grown tame in the silence that reigns
  around,
      Broken only, now and then,
By shy woodpecker or noisy jay,
By the far-off watch-dog's muffled bay;
      But where never the purposeless
      laughter of men,
  Or the seething city's murmurous sound
Will float up over the river-weeds.

Here may I live what life I please,
  Married and buried out of sight,—
      Married to pleasure, and buried to
      pain,—
Hidden away amongst scenes like these,
Under the fans of the chestnut trees;
      Living my child-life over again,
  With the further hope of a fallen delight,
Blithe as the birds and wise as the bees.

In green old gardens, hidden away
  From sight of revel and sound of strife,—

Here have I leisure to breathe and
move,
And to do my work in a nobler way;
To sing my songs, and to say my say;
To dream my dreams, and to love my
love;
To hold my faith, and to live my life.
Making the most of its shadowy day.

A Garden by the Sea

William Morris
1834–1896

I know a little garden-close,
Set thick with lily and red rose,
Where I would wander if I might
From dewy morn to dewy night,
And have one with me wandering.

And though within it no birds sing,
And though no pillared house is there,
And though the apple-boughs are bare
Of fruit and blossom, would to God
Her feet upon the green grass trod,
And I beheld them as before.

There comes a murmur from the shore,
And in the close two fair streams are,
Drawn from the purple hills afar,
Drawn down unto the restless sea:
Dark hills whose heath-bloom feeds no bee,
Dark shore no ship has ever seen,
Tormented by the billows green
Whose murmur comes unceasingly
Unto the place for which I cry.

For which I cry both day and night,
For which I let slip all delight,
Whereby I grow both deaf and blind,
Careless to win, unskilled to find,
And quick to lose what all men seek.

Yet tottering as I am and weak,
Still have I left a little breath
To seek within the jaws of death
An entrance to that happy place,
To seek the unforgotten face,
Once seen, once kissed, once reft from me
Anigh the murmuring of the sea.

From *"Visions"*

William Browne of Tavistock
1591–1643?

A rose, as fair as ever saw the north,
Grew in a little garden all alone;
A sweeter flower did Nature ne'er put forth,
Nor fairer garden yet was never known.
The maidens danced about it more and
    more,
And learned bards of it their ditties made;
The nimble fairies by the pale-faced moon
Watered the root and kissed her pretty
    shade.
But well-a-day, the gardener careless grew,
The maids and fairies both were kept away,
And in a drought the caterpillars threw
Themselves upon the bud and every spray.
God shield the stock! if Heaven send no
    supplies,
The fairest blossom of the garden dies.

Unguarded

Ada Foster Murray
1857–1936

The Mistress of the Roses
   Is haply far away,
And through her garden closes
   What strange intruders stray.

See on its rustic spindles
   The sundrop's amber fire!
And the goldenrod enkindles
   The embers on its spire.

The dodder's shining tangle
   From the meadow brook steals in,
Where in this shadowed angle
   The pale lace-makers spin.

Here's Black-Eyed Susan weeping
   Into exotic air,
And Bouncing Bet comes creeping
   Back to her old parterre.

Now in this pleasant weather—
So sweetly reconciled—
They dwell and dream together,
The kin of court and wild.

Song

Thomas Deloney
1563?–1600?

The primrose in the green forest,
  The violets, they be gay;
The double daisies, and the rest
  That trimly decks the way,
Doth move the spirits with brave delights,
  Who Beauty's darlings be:
With hey tricksy, trim-go-tricksy,
  Under the greenwood tree.

From *"Sonnets"*

Bartholomew Griffin
15—?–1602

Fair is my love that feeds among the lilies,
The lilies growing in that pleasant garden,
Where Cupid's mount, that well-beloved hill
   is,
And where the little god himself is warden.

See where my love sits in the bed of spices,
Beset all round with camphor, myrrh and
   roses,
And interlaced with curious devices,
Which her from all the world apart incloses.

My Garden Is a Pleasant Place

Louise Driscoll
1875–1957

My garden is a pleasant place
Of sun glory and leaf grace.
There is an ancient cherry tree
Where yellow warblers sing to me,
And an old grape arbor, where
A robin builds her nest, and there
Above the lima beans and peas
She croons her little melodies,
Her blue eggs hidden in the green
Fastness of that leafy screen.
Here are striped zinnias that bees
Fly far to visit; and sweet peas,
Like little butterflies newborn,
And over by the tasseled corn
Are sunflowers and hollyhocks,
And pink and yellow four-o'clocks.
Here are hummingbirds that come
To seek the tall delphinium—
Songless bird and scentless flower
Communing in a golden hour.

There is no blue like the blue cup
The tall delphinium holds up,
Not sky, nor distant hill, nor sea,
Sapphire, nor lapis lazuli.

My lilac trees are old and tall;
I cannot reach their bloom at all.
They send their perfume over trees
And roof and streets, to find the bees.

I wish some power would touch my ear
With magic touch, and make me hear
What all the blossoms say, and so
I might know what the winged things know.
I'd hear the sunflower's mellow pipe,
"Goldfinch, goldfinch, my seeds are ripe!"
I'd hear the pale wistaria sing,
"Moon moth, moon moth, I'm blossoming!"

I'd hear the evening primrose cry,
"Oh, firefly! come, firefly!"
And I would learn the jeweled word
The ruby-throated hummingbird
Drops into cups of larkspur blue,
And I would sing them all for you!

My garden is a pleasant place
Of moon glory and wind grace.
O friend, wherever you may be,
Will you not come to visit me?
Over fields and streams and hills,
I'll pipe like yellow daffodils,
And every little wind that blows
Shall take my message as it goes.
A heart may travel very far
To come where its desires are,
Oh, may some power touch my ear,
And grant me grace, and make you hear!

Who Loves a Garden

Louise Seymour Jones

Who loves a garden
Finds within his soul
Life's whole;
He hears the anthem of the soil
While ingrates toil;
And sees beyond his little sphere
The waving fronds of heaven, clear.

The Grass

Emily Dickinson
1830–1886

The grass so little has to do,—
    A sphere of simple green,
With only butterflies to brood,
    And bees to entertain,

And stir all day to pretty tunes
    The breezes fetch along,
And hold the sunshine in its lap
    And bow to everything;

And thread the dews all night, like pearls,
    And make itself so fine,—
A duchess were too common
    For such a noticing.

And even when it dies, to pass
    In odours so divine,
As lowly spices gone to sleep,
    Or amulets of pine.

The Voice of Grass

Sarah Roberts Boyle
1812–1869

Here I come creeping, creeping everywhere;
   By the dusty roadside,
   On the sunny hill-side,
   Close by the noisy brook,
   In every shady nook,
I come creeping, creeping everywhere.

Here I come creeping, smiling everywhere;
   All around the open door,
   Where sit the aged poor;
   Here where the children play.
   In the bright and merry May,
I come creeping, creeping everywhere.

Here I come creeping, creeping everywhere;
   In the noisy city street
   My pleasant face you'll meet,
   Cheering the sick at heart
   Toiling his busy part,—
Silently creeping, creeping everywhere.

Here I come creeping, creeping everywhere;
    You cannot see me coming,
    Nor hear my low sweet humming;
    For in the starry night,
    And the glad morning light,
I come quietly creeping everywhere.

Here I come creeping, creeping everywhere;
    More welcome than the flowers
    In summer's pleasant hours:
    The gentle cow is glad,
    And the merry bird not sad,
To see me creeping, creeping everywhere.

Here I come creeping, creeping everywhere:
    When you're numbered with the dead
    In your still and narrow bed,
    In the happy spring I'll come
    And deck your silent home—
Creeping, silently creeping everywhere.

Here I come creeping, creeping everywhere;
    My humble song of praise
    Most joyfully I raise
    To Him at whose command
    I beautify the land,
Creeping, silently creeping everywhere.

To Meadows

Robert Herrick
1591–1674

Ye have been fresh and green,
    Ye have been filled with flowers;
And ye the walks have been
    Where maids have spent their hours.

You have beheld how they
    With wicker arks did come,
To kiss and bear away
    The richer cowslips home.

Ye've heard them sweetly sing,
    And seen them in a round;
Each virgin, like a spring,
    With honeysuckles crowned.

But now, we see none here
    Whose silvery feet did tread,
And with dishevelled hair
    Adorned this smoother mead.

Like unthrifts, having spent
    Your stock, and needy grown,
Ye're left here to lament
    Your poor estates, alone.

The Genesis of Butterflies

Victor Hugo
1802–1885

The dawn is smiling on the dew that covers
The tearful roses; lo, the little lovers
That kiss the buds, and all the flutterings
In jasmine bloom, and privet, of white wings,
That go and come, and fly, and peep and
    hide,
With muffled music, murmured far and
    wide.
Ah, the Spring time, when we think of all
    the lays
That dreamy lovers send to dreamy mays,
Of the fond hearts within a billet bound,
Of all the soft silk paper that pens wound,
The messages of love that mortals write
Filled with intoxication of delight,
Written in April and before the May time
Shredded and flown, playthings for the
    wind's playtime,
We dream that all white butterflies above,
Who seek through clouds or waters souls to
    love,

And leave their lady mistress in despair,
To flit to flowers, as kinder and more fair,
Are but torn love-letters, that through the
skies
Flutter, and float, and change to butterflies.

Translated by Andrew Lang

Fireflies in the Garden

Robert Frost
1874–1963

Here come real stars to fill the upper skies,
And here on earth come emulating flies,
That though they never equal stars in size,
(And they were never really stars at heart)
Achieve at times a very star-like start.
Only, of course, they can't sustain the part.

From *"The Parliament of Bees"*

John Day
1574?–1640?

Vintager: High steward of thy vines,
Taster both of grapes and wines,
In these ripe clusters present
Full bounty, on his knees low
    bent,
Pays Oberon homage; and in this
    bowl
Brimmed with grape blood, tender
    toll
Of all thy vintage.

Oberon: May thy grapes thrive
In autumn, and the roots survive
In churlish winter; may thy fence
Be proof 'gainst wild boars'
    violence;
As thou in service true shalt be
To us and our high royalty.
—A female bee: thy character?

Flora:	Flora, Oberon's gardener,
	(Housewife both of herbs and
	flowers,
	To strew thy shrine and trim thy
	bowers
	With violets, roses, eglantine,
	Daffodil and blue columbine)
	Hath forth the bosom of the
	spring
	Plucked this nosegay, which I
	bring
	From Eleusis, mine own shrine,
	To thee a monarch all divine;
	And, as true impost of my grove,
	Present it to great Oberon's love.
Oberon:	Honey-dew refresh thy meads,
	Cowslips spring with golden
	heads;
	July-flowers and carnations wear
	Leaves double streaked with
	maiden-hair;
	May thy lilies taller grow,
	Thy violets fuller sweetness owe;
	And, last of all, may Phoebus
	love
	To kiss thee and frequent thy
	grove,
	As thou in service true shalt be
	Unto our crown and royalty.

The Pedigree of Honey

Emily Dickinson
1830–1886

The pedigree of honey
Does not concern the bee;
A clover, any time, to him,
Is aristocracy.

Where the Bee Sucks

From "The Tempest"

William Shakespeare
1564–1616

Where the bee sucks, there suck I:
In a cowslip's bell I lie;
There I couch when owls do cry.
On the bat's back I do fly
After summer merrily.
Merrily, merrily shall I live now
Under the blossom that hangs on the bough.

A Widow's Weeds

Walter de la Mare
1873–1956

A poor old Widow in her weeds
Sowed her garden with wild-flower seeds;
Not too shallow, and not too deep,
And down came April—drip—drip—drip.
Up shone May, like gold, and soon
Green as an arbour grew leafy June.
And now all summer she sits and sews
Where willow herb, comfrey, bugloss blows,
Teasle and tansy, meadowsweet,
Campion, toadflax, and rough hawksbit;
Brown bee orchis, and Peals of Bells;
Clover, burnet, and thyme she smells;
Like Oberon's meadows her garden is
Drowsy from dawn till dusk with bees.
Weeps she never, but sometimes sighs,
And peeps at her garden with bright brown
    eyes;
And all she has is all she needs—
A poor old Widow in her weeds.

"Long Live the Weeds"

Theodore Roethke
1908–1963

Long live the weeds that overwhelm
My narrow vegetable realm!
The bitter rock, the barren soil
That force the son of man to toil;
All things unholy, marred by curse,
The ugly of the universe.
The rough, the wicked, and the wild
That keep the spirit undefiled.
With these I match my little wit
And earn the right to stand or sit.
Hope, love, create, or drink and die:
These shape the creature that is I.

A Day in June
From "The Vision of Sir Launfal"

James Russell Lowell
1819–1891

And what is so rare as a day in June?
   Then, if ever, come perfect days;
Then Heaven tries earth if it be in tune,
   And over it softly her warm ear lays;
Whether we look, or whether we listen,
   We hear life murmur, or see it glisten;
Every clod feels a stir of might,
   An instinct within it that reaches and
     towers,
And, groping blindly above it for light,
   Climbs to a soul in grass and flowers.

Afternoon on a Hill

Edna St. Vincent Millay
1892–1950

I will be the gladdest thing
    Under the sun!
I will touch a hundred flowers
    And not pick one.

I will look at cliffs and clouds
    With quiet eyes,
Watch the wind bow down the grass,
    And the grass rise.

And when lights begin to show
    Up from the town,
I will mark which must be mine,
    And then start down!

Noon

Michael Field
(Katharine Bradley, 1846–1914, and
Edith Cooper, 1862–1913)

Full summer and at noon; from a waste bed
Convolvulus, musk-mallow, poppies spread
The triumph of the sunshine overhead.

Blue on refulgent ash-trees lies the heat;
It tingles on the hedge-rows; the young
    wheat
Sleeps, warm in golden verdure, at my feet.

The pale, sweet grasses of the hayfield blink;
The heath-moors, as the bees of honey
    drink,
Suck the deep bosom of the day. To think

Of all that beauty by the light defined
None shares my vision! Sharply on my mind
Presses the sorrow: fern and flower are
    blind.

Flower in the Crannied Wall

Alfred, Lord Tennyson
1809–1892

Flower in the crannied wall,
I pluck you out of the crannies,
I hold you here, root and all, in my hand,
Little flower—but *if* I could understand
What you are, root and all, and all in all,
I should know what God and man is.

Child on Top of a Greenhouse

Theodore Roethke
1908–1963

The wind billowing out the seat of my
 britches,
My feet crackling splinters of glass and dried
 putty,
The half-grown chrysanthemums staring up
 like accusers,
Up through the streaked glass, flashing with
 sunlight,
A few white clouds all rushing eastward,
A line of elms plunging and tossing like
 horses,
And everyone, everyone pointing up and
 shouting!

Window Boxes

Eleanor Farjeon
1881–1965

A window box of pansies
   Is such a happy thing.
A window box of wallflowers
   Is a garden for a king.
A window box of roses
   Makes everyone stand still
Who sees a garden growing
   On a window sill.

Window Ledge in the Atom Age

E. B. White
1899–1985

I have a bowl of paper whites,
  Of paper-white narcissus;
Their fragrance my whole soul delights,
  They smell delissus.
      (They grow in pebbles in the sun
        And each is like a star.)

I sit and scan the news hard by
  My paper-white narcissus;
I read how fast a plane can fly,
  Against my wissus.
      (The course of speed is almost run,
        We know not where we are.)

They grow in pebbles in the sun,
  My beautiful narcissus,
Casting their subtle shade upon
  Tropical fissus.
      (No movement mars each tiny star;
        Speed has been left behind.)

I'd gladly trade the latest thing
  For paper-white narcissus;
Science, upon its airfoil wing,
  Now seems pernissus.
    (Who was it said to travel far
      Might dissipate the mind?)

I love this day, this hour, this room,
  This motionless narcissus;
I love the stillness of the home,
  I love the missus.
    (She grows in pebbles in my sun
      And she is like a star.)

And though the modern world be through
  With paper-white narcissus,
I shall arise and I shall do
  The breakfast dissus.
    (The tranquil heart may yet outrun
      The rocket and the car.)

The Wreath

Meleager
75 B.C.–?

Now will I weave white violets, daffodils
   With myrtle spray,
And lily bells that trembling laughter fills,
   And the sweet crocus gay:
With these blue hyacinth, and the lover's
     rose
   That she may wear—
My sun-maiden—each scented flower that
    blows,
   Upon her scented hair.

Translated by William M. Hardinge

A Garden Song

George R. Sims
1847–1922

I scorn the doubts and cares that hurt
   The world and all its mockeries,
My only care is now to squirt
   The ferns among my rockeries.

In early youth and later life
   I've seen an up and seen a down,
And now I have a loving wife
   To help me peg verbena down.

Of joys that come to womankind
   The loom of fate doth weave her few,
But here are summer joys entwined
   And bound with golden feverfew,

I've learnt the lessons one and all
   With which the world its sermon stocks,
Now, heedless of a rise or fall,
   I've Brompton and I've German stocks.

In peace and quiet pass our days,
    With nought to vex our craniums,
Our middle beds are all ablaze
    With red and white geraniums.

And like a boy I laugh when she,
    In Varden hat and Varden hose,
Comes slyly up the lawn at me
    To squirt me with the garden hose.

Let him who'd have the peace he needs
    Give all his worldly mumming up,
Then dig a garden, plant the seeds,
    And watch the product coming up.

Come into the Garden, Maud

Alfred, Lord Tennyson
1809–1892

Come into the garden, Maud,
   For the black bat, night, has flown,
Come into the garden, Maud,
   I am here at the gate alone;
And the woodbine spices are wafted abroad,
   And the musk of the rose is blown.

For a breeze of morning moves,
   And the planet of Love is on high,
Beginning to faint in the light that she loves
   On a bed of daffodil sky,
To faint in the light of the sun she loves,
   To faint in his light, and to die.

All night have the roses heard
   The flute, violin, bassoon;
All night has the casement jessamine stirred
   To the dancers dancing in tune;
Till a silence fell with the waking bird,
   And a hush with the setting moon.

I said to the lily, "There is but one
 With whom she has heart to be gay.
When will the dancers leave her alone?
 She is weary of dance and play."
Now half to the setting moon are gone,
 And half to the rising day;
Low on the sand and loud on the stone
 The last wheel echoes away.

I said to the rose, "The brief night goes
 In babble and revel and wine.
O young lord-lover, what sighs are those,
 For one that will never be thine?
But mine, but mine," so I sware to the rose,
 "For ever and ever, mine."

And the soul of the rose went into my blood,
 As the music clashed in the hall;
And long by the garden lake I stood,
 For I heard your rivulet fall
From the lake to the meadow and on to the
  wood,
 Our wood, that is dearer than all;

From the meadow your walks have left so
  sweet
 That whenever a March-wind sighs
He sets the jewel-print of your feet
 In violets blue as your eyes,

To the woody hollows in which we meet
    And the valleys of Paradise.

The slender acacia would not shake
    One long milk-bloom on the tree;
The white lake-blossom fell into the lake
    As the pimpernel dozed on the lea;
But the rose was awake all night for your
        sake,
    Knowing your promise to me;
The lilies and roses were all awake,
    They sighed for the dawn and thee.

Queen rose of the rosebud garden of girls,
    Come hither, the dances are done,
In glass of satin and glimmer of pearls,
    Queen lily and rose in one;
Shine out, little head, sunning over with
        curls,
    To the flowers, and be their sun.

There has fallen a splendid tear
    From the passion-flower at the gate.
She is coming, my dove, my dear;
    She is coming, my life, my fate;
The red rose cries, "She is near, she is near";
    And the white rose weeps, "She is late";
The larkspur listens, "I hear, I hear";
    And the lily whispers, "I wait."

She is coming, my own, my sweet,
　Were it ever so airy a tread,
My heart would hear her and beat,
　Were it earth in an earthy bed;
My dust would hear her and beat,
　Had I lain for a century dead;
Would start and tremble under her feet,
　And blossom in purple and red.

The Tryst

John B. Tabb
1845–1909

Potato was deep in the dark under ground,
   Tomato, above in the light.
The little Tomato was ruddy and round,
   The little Potato was white.

And redder and redder she rounded above,
   And paler and paler he grew,
And neither suspected a mutual love
   Till they met in a Brunswick stew.

Vegetables

Eleanor Farjeon
1881–1965

The country vegetables scorn
    To lie about in shops,
They stand upright as they were born
    In neatly-patterned crops;

And when you want your dinner you
    Don't buy it from a shelf,
You find a lettuce fresh with dew
    And pull it for yourself;

You pick an apronful of peas
    And shell them on the spot.
You cut a cabbage, if you please,
    To pop into the pot.

The folk who their potatoes buy
    From sacks before they sup,
Miss half of the potato's joy
    And that's to dig it up.

For Instance

From "Contributions"

Robert McAlmon
1895–1956

Vegetables

and jewelry, rightly displayed,
have an equal amount of fascination.

Carrots, for instance,
piled—
ferntops, bodies, and hair roots
so bound together in bunches—
bunches laid in rows
of oblong heaps with magnitude,
are sufficient to arrest any seeing eye.

Cabbages with a purplish tinge,
when of grandeur, with widespread petals,
as they rest in heaps
catching the dawn's first filtering of sunlight,
compare satisfyingly with roses enmassed,
with orchids, sunflowers, tulips,
or variegated flowers
extravagantly scattered.

While as to onions,
little can excel their decorative effect
when green tubes, white bulbs, and grey hair
   roots
rest in well arranged, paralleled piles
about which buxom women congregate,
laughing and chattering in wholesome
   vulgarity.

Crispness,
a cool indifference to the gash of knives,
to the crush of kind,
or to any destiny whatsoever,
has granted the vegetables an arrogance of
   identity
one would be foolhardy to strive after
with heated impressionable imagination.

Vegetables,
given their color,
scent and freshness,
too easily attain a cool supremacy of being
for our fumbling competition.

The Love of Lettuce

Marge Piercy
1936–

With a pale green curly
lust I gloat over it nestled
there on the wet earth
(oakleaf, buttercrunch, ruby, cos)
like so many nests
waiting for birds
who lay hard boiled eggs.

The first green eyes
of the mustard, the frail
wands of carrots, the fat
thrust of the peas: all
are precious as I kneel
in the mud weeding
and the thinnings go into the salad.

The garden with crooked
wandering rows dug
by the three of us
drunk with sunshine has
an intricate pattern emerging
like the back of a rug.
The tender seedlings

raise their pinheads
with the cap of seed stuck on.
Cruel and smiling with sharp
teeth is the love of lettuce.
You grow out of last year's
composted dinner and you
will end up in my hot mouth.

How to Grow Cucumbers
From "The Task"

William Cowper
1731–1800

The stable yields a stercoraceous heap,
Impregnated with quick fermenting salts,
And potent to resist the freezing blast:
For ere the beech and elm have cast their
    leaf
Deciduous, when now November dark
Checks vegetation in the torpid plant
Exposed to his cold breath, the task begins.
Warily therefore, and with prudent heed,
He seeks a favour's spot; that where he
    builds
The agglomerated pile, his frame may front
The sun's meridan disk, and at the back
Enjoy close shelter, wall, or reeds, or hedge
Impervious to the wind. First he bids spread
Dry fern or litter'd hay, that may imbibe
The ascending damps, then leisurely impose,
And lightly shaking it with agile hand
Form the full fork, the saturated straw.
What longest binds the closest, forms secure

The shapely side, that as it rises takes,
By just degrees, an over-hanging breadth,
Sheltering the base with its projected eaves.
The uplifted frame compact at every joint,
And overlaid with clear translucent glass,
He settles next upon the sloping mount,
Whose sharp declivity shoots off secure
From the dash'd pane the deluge as it falls:
He shuts it close, and the first labour ends.

The seed, selected wisely, plump, and
    smooth,
And glossy, he commits to pots of size
Diminutive, well filled with well-prepared
And fruitful soil, that has been treasured
    long
And drank no moisture from the dripping
    clouds:
These on the warm and genial earth that
    hides
The smoking manure, and o'erspreads it all,
He places lightly, and as time subdues
The rage of fermentation, plunges deep
In the soft medium, till they stand
    immersed.
Then rise the tender germs, upstarting quick
And spreading wide their spongy lobes, at
    first

Place, wan, and livid, but assuming soon,
If fann'd by balmy nutritious air,
Strain'd through the friendly mats, a vivid
    green.
Two leaves produced, two rough indented
    leaves,
Cautious he pinches from the second stalk
A pimple, that portends a future sprout,
And interdicts its growth. Thence straight
    succeed
The branches, sturdy to his utmost wish,
Prolific all, and harbingers of more.
The crowded roots demand enlargement now,
And transplantation in an ampler space.
Indulged in what they wish, they soon supply
Large foliage, overshadowing golden flowers,
Blown on the summit of the apparent fruit.
These have their sexes, and when summer
    shines
The bee transports the fertilising meal
From flower to flower, and even the
    breathing air
Wafts the rich prize to its appointed use.
Not so when winter scowls. Assistant art
Then acts in Nature's office, brings to pass
The glad espousals, and ensures the crop.

Summer Dawn

William Morris
1834–1896

Pray but one prayer for me 'twixt thy closed
    lips,
  Think but one thought of me up in the
    stars.
The summer night waneth, the morning light
    slips,
  Faint & grey 'twixt the leaves of the
    aspen, betwixt the cloud-bars,
That are patiently waiting there for the
    dawn:
  Patient and colourless, though Heaven's
    gold
Waits to float through them along with the
    sun.
Far out in the meadows, above the young
    corn,
  The heavy elms wait, and restless and cold
The uneasy wind rises; the roses are dun;

Through the long twilight they pray for the
  dawn,
Round the lone house in the midst of the
  corn.
  Speak but one word to me over the corn,
  Over the tender, bow'd locks of the corn.

Korosta Katzina Song

Hopi

1

Yellow butterflies
Over the blossoming virgin corn,
 With pollen-painted faces
Chase one another in brilliant throng.

2

Blue butterflies
Over the blossoming virgin beans,
 With pollen-painted faces
Chase one another in brilliant streams.

3

Over the blossoming corn,
Over the virgin corn,
Wild bees hum;
Over the blossoming corn,
Over the virgin beans
Wild bees hum.

4

Over your field of growing corn
All day shall hang the thunder-cloud;
Over your field of growing corn
All day shall come the rushing rain.

Translated by Natalie Curtis

The Voice that Beautifies the Land

Navaho

1

The voice that beautifies the land!
The voice above,
The voice of the thunder,
Among the dark clouds
Again and again it sounds,
The voice that beautifies the land.

2

The voice that beautifies the land!
The voice below,
The voice of the grasshopper,
Among the flowers and grasses
Again and again it sounds,
The voice that beautifies the land.

Translated by Washington Matthews

Thy Garden

Mu'tamid, King of Seville
1040–1095

My thoughts are as a garden-plot, that knows
No rain but of thy giving, and no rose
Except thy name. I dedicate it thine,
My garden, full of fruits in harvest time.

The Harvest

Alice C. Henderson
1881–1949

The silver rain, the shining sun,
The fields where scarlet poppies run,
And all the ripples of the wheat
Are in the bread that I do eat.

So when I sit for every meal
And say a grace, I always feel
That I am eating rain and sun,
And fields where scarlet poppies run.

Trees

Joyce Kilmer
1886–1918

I think that I shall never see
A poem lovely as a tree.

A tree whose hungry mouth is pressed
Against the earth's sweet flowing breast;

A tree that looks at God all day
And lifts her leafy arms to pray;

A tree that may in summer wear
A nest of robins in her hair;

Upon whose bosom snow has lain;
Who intimately lives with rain.

Poems are made by fools like me,
But only God can make a tree.

In the Orchard

Henrik Ibsen
1828–1906

In the sunny orchard closes,
   While the warblers sing and swing,
Care not whether blustering Autumn
   Break the promises of Spring!
Rose and white, the apple blossom
   Hides you from the sultry sky—
Let it flutter, blown and scatter'd,
   On the meadows by-and-by!

Will you ask about the fruitage
   In the season of the flowers?
Will you murmur, will you question,
   Count the run of weary hours?
Will you let the scarecrow clapping
   Drown all happy sounds and words?
Brothers! there is better music
   In the singing of the birds.

From your heavy-laden garden
   Will you hunt the mellow thrush:
He will play you for protection
   With his crown-song's liquid rush.
O but you will win the bargain,
   Though your fruit be spare and late,
For remember Time is flying
   And will shut the garden gate.

With my living, with my singing,
   I will tear the hedges down.
Sweep the grass and heap the blossom!
   Let it shrivel, pale and brown!
Swing the wicket! Sheep and cattle,
   Let them graze among the best!
I broke off the flowers; what matter
   Who may revel with the rest?

Translated by Sir Edmund Gosse

The Wild Honey Suckle

Philip Freneau
1752–1832

Fair flower, that dost so comely grow,
Hid in this silent, dull retreat,
Untouched thy honied blossoms blow,
Unseen thy little branches greet:
    No roving foot shall crush thee here,
    No busy hand provoke a tear.

By Nature's self in white arrayed,
She bade thee shun the vulgar eye,
And planted here the guardian shade,
And sent soft waters murmuring by;
    Thus quietly thy summer goes,
    Thy days declining to repose.

Smit with those charms, that must decay,
I grieve to see your future doom;
They died—nor were those flowers more gay,
The flowers that did in Eden bloom;
    Unpitying frosts, and Autumn's power
    Shall leave no vestige of this flower.

From morning suns and evening dews
At first thy little being came:
If nothing once, you nothing lose,
For when you die you are the same;
    The space between, is but an hour,
    The frail duration of a flower.

A Spray of Honeysuckle

Mary Emily Bradley
1835–1898

I broke one day a slender stem,
   Thick-set with little golden horns,
Half bud, half blossom, and a gem—
   Such as one finds in autumn morns
When all the grass with dew is strung—
On every fairy bugle hung.

Careless, I dropped it, in a place
   Where no light shone, and so forgot
Its delicate, dewy, flowering grace,
   Till presently from the dark spot
A charming sense of sweetness came,
That woke an answering sense of shame.

Quickly I thought, O heart of mine,
   A lesson for thee plain to read:
Thou needest not that light should shine,
   Or fellow-men thy virtues heed:
Enough—if haply this be so—
That thou hast sweetness to bestow!

Goldenrod

Elaine Goodale Eastman

When the wayside tangles blaze
    In the low September sun,
When the flowers of Summer days
    Droop and wither, one by one,
Reaching up through bush and brier,
Sumptuous brow and heart of fire,
Flaunting high its wind-rocked plume,
Brave with wealth of native bloom,—
        Goldenrod!

When the meadow, lately shorn,
    Parched and languid, swoons with pain,
When her life-blood, night and morn,
    Shrinks in every throbbing vein,
Round her fallen, tarnished urn
Leaping watch-fires brighter burn;
Royal arch o'er Autumn's gate,
Bending low with lustrous weight,—
        Goldenrod!

In the pasture's rude embrace,
  All o'errun with tangled vines,
Where the thistle claims its place,
  And the straggling hedge confines,
Bearing still the sweet impress,
Of unfettered loveliness,
In the field and by the wall,
Binding, clasping, crowning all,—
      Goldenrod!

Nature lies dishevelled, pale,
  With her feverish lips apart,—
Day by day the pulses fail,
  Nearer to her bounding heart;
Yet that slackened grasp doth hold
Store of pure and genuine gold;
Quick thou comest, strong and free,
Type of all the wealth to be,—
      Goldenrod!

Round the Year

Coventry Patmore
1823–1896

The Crocus, while the days are dark,
  Unfolds its saffron sheen;
At April's touch, the crudest bark
  Discovers germs of green.

Then sleep the seasons, full of might;
  While swells the pod
And rounds the peach, and in the night
  The mushroom bursts the sod.

The winter falls; the frozen rut
  Is bound with silver bars,
The snowdrift heaps against the hut
  And night is pierced with stars.

The Last Rose of Summer

Thomas Moore
1779–1852

'Tis the last rose of summer
 Left blooming alone;
All her lovely companions
 Are faded and gone;
No flower of her kindred,
 No rose-bud is nigh,
To reflect back her blushes,
 Or give sigh for sigh.

I'll not leave thee, thou lone one!
 To pine on the stem;
Since the lovely are sleeping,
 Go, sleep thou with them.
Thus kindly I scatter
 Thy leaves o'er the bed
Where thy mates of the garden
 Lie scentless and dead.

So soon may I follow,
  When friendships decay,
And from Love's shining circle
  The gems drop away.
When true hearts lie withered,
  And fond ones are flown,
O! who would inhabit
  This bleak world alone?

Cyclamens

Michael Field
(Katharine Bradley, 1846–1914, and
Edith Cooper, 1862–1913)

They are terribly white:
There is snow on the ground,
   And a moon on the snow at night;
   The sky is cut by the winter light;
Yet I, who have all these things in ken,
Am struck to the heart by the chiselled
     white
   Of this handful of cyclamen.

The White Chrysanthemum

Oshikochi no Mitsune
c. 900

The white chrysanthemum
Is disguised by the first frost.
If I wanted to pick one
I could find it only by chance.

Translated by Kenneth Rexroth

Pumpkins

John Cotton
1925–

At the end of the garden,
Across the litter of weeds and grass cuttings,
The pumpkin spreads its coarse,
Bristled, hollow-stemmed lines,
Erupting in great leaves
Above flowers
The nobbly and prominent
Stigmas of which
Are like fuses
Waiting to be set by bees.

When, like a string
Of yellow mines
Across the garden,
The pumpkins will smolder
And swell,
Drawing the combustion from the sun
To make their own.

At night I lie
Waiting for detonations,
Half expecting
To find the garden
Cratered like a moon.

An Autumn Garden

Bliss Carman
1861–1929

My tent stands in a garden
Of aster and golden-rod,
Tilled by the rain and the sunshine,
And sown by the hand of God,—
An old New England pasture
Abandoned to peace and time,
And by the magic of beauty
Reclaimed to the sublime.

About it are golden woodlands
Of tulip and hickory;
On the open ridge behind it
You may mount to a glimpse of sea,—
The far-off, blue, Homeric
Rim of the world's great shield,
A border of boundless glamor
For the soul's familiar field.

In purple and gray-wrought lichen
The boulders lie in the sun;
Along its grassy footpath,
The white-tailed rabbits run.
The crickets work and chirrup
Through the still afternoon;
And the owl calls at twilight
Under the frosty moon.

The odorous wild grape clambers
Over the tumbling wall,
And through the autumnal quiet
The chestnuts open and fall.
Sharing time's freshness and fragrance,
Part of the earth's great soul,
Here man's spirit may ripen
To wisdom serene and whole.

Shall we not grow with the asters?—
Never reluctant nor sad,
Not counting the cost of being,
Living to dare and be glad.
Shall we not lift with the crickets
A chorus or ready cheer,
Braving the frost of oblivion,
Quick to be happy here?

The deep red cones of the sumach
And the woodbine's crimson sprays
Have bannered the common roadside
For the pageant of passing days.
These are the oracles Nature
Fills with her holy breath,
Giving them glory of color,
Transcending the shadow of death.

Here in the sifted sunlight
A spirit seems to brood
On the beauty and worth of being,
In tranquil, instinctive mood
And the heart, athrob with gladness
Such as the wise earth knows,
Wells with a full thanksgiving
For the gifts that life bestows:

For the ancient and virile nurture
Of the teeming primordial ground,
For the splendid gospel of color,
The rapt revelations of sound;
For the morning-blue above us
And the rusted gold of the fern,
For the chickadee's call to valor
Bidding the faint-heart turn;

For fire and running water,
Snowfall and summer rain;
For sunsets and quiet meadows,
The fruit and the standing grain;
For the solemn hour of moonrise
Over the crest of trees,
When the mellow lights are kindled
In the lamps of the centuries.

For those who wrought aforetime,
Led by the mystic strain
To strive for the larger freedom,
And live for the greater gain;
For plenty and peace and playtime,
The homely goods of earth,
And for rare immaterial treasures
Accounted of little worth;

For art and learning and friendship,
Where beneficent truth is supreme,
Those everlasting cities
Built on the hills of dream;
For all things growing and goodly
That foster this life, and breed
The immortal flower of wisdom
Out of the mortal seed.

But most of all for the spirit
That can not rest nor bide
In stale and sterile convenience,
Nor safety proven and tried,
But still inspired and driven,
Must seek what better may be,
And up from the loveliest garden
Must climb for a glimpse of sea.

The Garden
From *"October Poems"*
On a Fine Day in Early Autumn

Robert Penn Warren
1905–1989

How kind, how secretly, the sun
Has blessed this garden frost has won,
And touched again, as once it used,
The furled boughs by frost bemused.
Though summered brilliance had but
    room
For blossom, now the leaves will bloom
Their time, and take from a milder sun
The unreviving benison.

No marbles whitely gleam among
These paths where gilt the late pear hung;
But branches interlace to frame
An avenue of stately flame
Where yonder, far more chill and pure
Than marble, gleams the sycamore,
Of argent torse and cunning shaft
Propped nobler than the sculptor's craft.

The hand that crooked upon the spade
Here plucked the peach, and thirst allayed;
Here lovers paused upon the kiss,
Instructed of what ripeness is.
Where all who came might stand to try
The grace of this green empery.
Now jay and cardinal debate,
Like twin usurpers, the ruined state.

Then he who sought, not love but peace,
In such rank plot could take no ease:
Now poised between the two alarms
Of summer's lusts and winter's harms,
For him alone these precincts wait
With sacrament that could translate
All things that fed luxurious sense
From appetite to innocence.

From "The Burning of the Leaves"

Laurence Binyon
1869–1943

Now is the time for the burning of the
   leaves,
They go to the fire: the nostril pricks with
   smoke
Wandering slowly into a weeping mist.
Brittle and blotched, ragged and rotten
   sheaves!
A flame seizes the smouldering ruin and
   bites
On stubborn stalks that crackle as they
   resist.

The last hollyhock's fallen tower is dust;
All the spices of June are a bitter reek,
All the extravagant riches spent and mean.
All burns! The reddest rose is a ghost;
Sparks whirl up, to expire in the mist: the
   wild
Fingers of fire are making corruption clean.

Now is the time for stripping the spirit bare,
Time for the burning of days ended and
 done,
Idle solace of things that have gone before:
Rootless hope and fruitless desire are there;
Let them go to the fire, with never a look
 behind.
The world that was ours is a world that is
 ours no more.

They will come again, the leaf and the
 flower, to arise
From squalor of rottenness into the old
 splendour,
And magical scents to a wondering memory
 bring;
The same glory, to shine upon different eyes.
Earth cares for her own ruins, naught for
 ours.
Nothing is certain, only the certain spring.

The First Blue-Bird

James Whitcomb Riley
1849–1916

Jest rain and snow! and rain again!
　　And dribble! drip! and blow!
Then snow! and thaw! and slush! and then—
　　Some more rain and snow!

This morning I was 'most afeard
　　To *wake* up—when, I jing!
I seen the sun shine out and heerd
　　The first blue-bird of Spring!—
Mother she'd raised the winder some;—
And in acrost the orchard come,
　　Soft as an angel's wing,
A breezy, treesy, beesy hum,
　　Too sweet for any thing!

The winter's shroud was rent apart—
　　The sun bust forth in glee,—
And when *that blue-bird* sung, my hart
　　Hopped out o' bed with me!

Index of Titles

191

Index of Poets and Translators